The oh so so-so Kakapo

Dan Douglass

Illustrations by Daniel Egneus

TWO

TALES
FOR THE
BIRDS

The oh so so-so kakapo

BY DAN DOUGLASS

Story by: **Dan Douglass**
Illustrations by: **Daniel Egneus**
Design by: **David Penn**

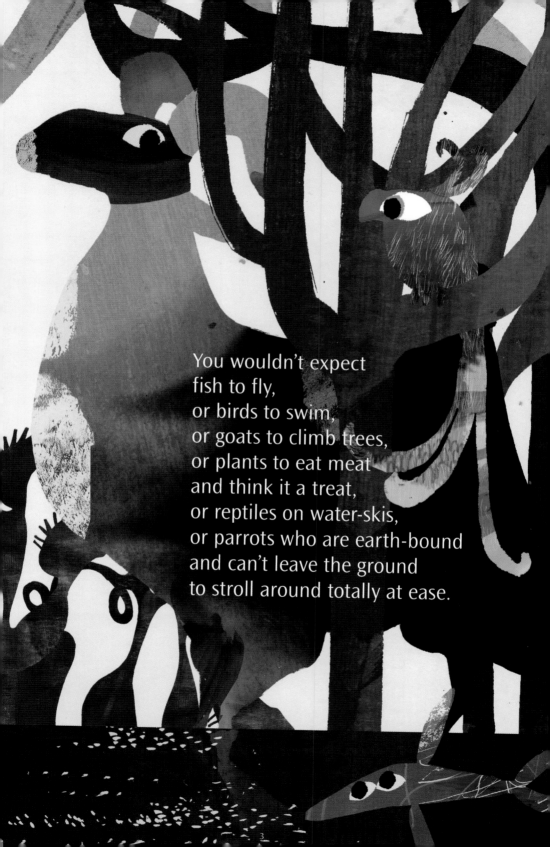

You wouldn't expect
fish to fly,
or birds to swim,
or goats to climb trees,
or plants to eat meat
and think it a treat,
or reptiles on water-skis,
or parrots who are earth-bound
and can't leave the ground
to stroll around totally at ease.

So how do you explain
a flying fish,
a dive-bombing penguin,
a goat up a tree
(or even a whole herd!),

a Venus fly-trap,
a Jesus Christ lizard,
whose waterborne sprints look absurd,
or the flightless kakapo,
who hikes, don't you know -
a shambling, ambling bird!

The southern hemisphere's home to birds
who are flightless and not so nimble.
The ostrich, the reah, the emu, the kiwi -
New Zealand's national symbol.

But a parrot who lives on the ground,
where other birds dare not risk it,
is a sight to see. All the parrots agree,
"This kakapo takes the biscuit".

What's more, say the parrots, the kakapo
is lucky to be here at all.
For in life he'd much rather go solo,
despite his strange mating call.

His gait is hardly athletic.
He has no real get up and go.
He acts like he just can't be bothered -
the so-so kakapo.

He's a bumbling old thing, say the parrots,
and his life skills are terribly bad.
To his mate, he's a complete and utter state.
To his chicks, he's an absentee Dad.

But let's not just rely for our truth
on what other parrots opine.
When it comes to survival techniques,
this kakapo would have been fine.

Born in the land of the kiwi,
Colin the kakapo roamed supreme,
for this bird had a camouflage suit on -
the best that had never been seen.

On these friendly, peaceful islands,
flying bats were his only real foe.
There were no other mammals to harm him -
Colin the kakapo.

Given the bats were airborne
and more of a threat in the sky,
Colin took to the forest floor
and waved aerobatics goodbye.

Far from sporting rainbow plumage,
like a loud proud Maori chief,
Colin was browny-green all over
to blend in with earth, moss and leaf.

He'd no need for bright coloured feathers,
for time and time again,
he'd go walking about at dead of night
and what use is gay plumage then?

Without any aerial exertions,
it's true Colin let himself go.
He ballooned to a full eight pounds -
the flabby kakapo.

But he needed his fat to store food
whilst wintering on the floor.
There's not a lot of tuck down there,
so he decided to forage for more.

Colin climbed the rimu tree
to pick the tastiest fruit,
then floated down with wings unfurled,
just like a parachute.

Because he jogged, his legs
became all muscular and short.
He looked more like a small capybara -
a feathery, beaky sort.

If threatened by a flying bat,
he neither fought nor fled,
but did something most peculiar.
He froze to the spot instead.

Colin kept himself to himself
with other kakapos around,
and if one was about, he'd let out
a chill shrill skraarking sound.

KARK!.

But needs must when it comes to the future.
For all animals it has to be done.
If you want to ensure you're survived by more,
you can't just stay as one.

He was a bit of a loner was Colin.
But for kakapos, when push comes to shove,
the survival instinct is stronger.
So he searched for his true lady love.

He gave off a terrible musty smell
with which he was wont to woo.
Truth to tell, this was all very well,
but the whole forest smelt him too.

Colin then dated and mated
by lowering his owlish head,
and, once his chest had inflated,
he'd call "boom!" for a beauty to wed.

He'd "boom!" a thousand times an hour,
up to seven hours a night.
Every night for three months,
he cut the most ludicrous sight.

At the end of this mating marathon,
Colin was on his knees.
He'd lost half his body weight "booming",
and his neighbours weren't very pleased.

But he'd found his Mrs Kakapo
and she soon had chicks to protect.
So you could say his noisy courtship
had the desired effect.

But then men came to the islands
who brought dogs, rats and hunger.
Colin now had to find a plan 'B'
(he wasn't getting any younger).

So this flightless bird thought of something
no land mammal had in mind.
He would teach his family to fly
and leave the ground far behind.

He wasn't a lemming, far from it.
He was driven by hope, not despair.
He just wanted to know he could fly himself
before his family took to the air.

So he walked to a point at the clifftop
where land and sea meet the sky.
Colin looked to the heavens with wonder
and waved the good earth goodbye.

Some said he was daft to attempt it.
Others thought he was brave to try.
But there's a drunk macaw who once swore he saw
a kakapo flying by.

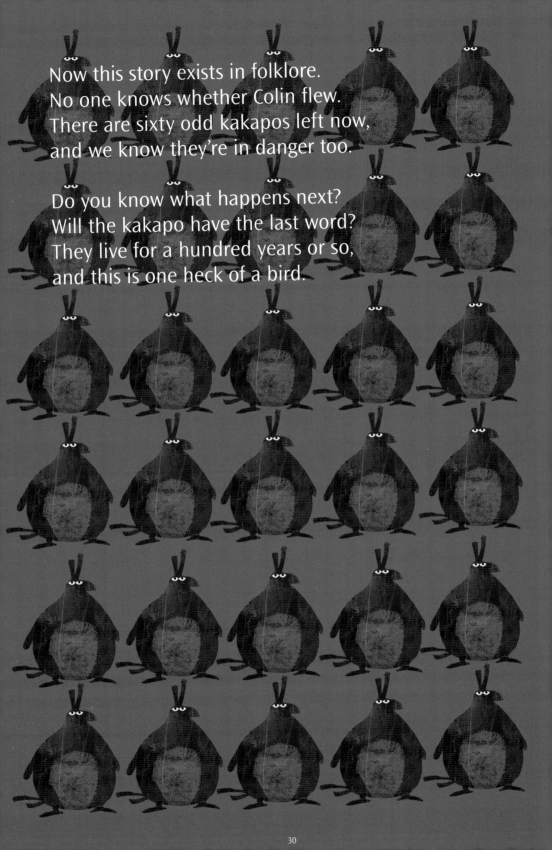

Now this story exists in folklore.
No one knows whether Colin flew.
There are sixty odd kakapos left now,
and we know they're in danger too.

Do you know what happens next?
Will the kakapo have the last word?
They live for a hundred years or so,
and this is one heck of a bird.

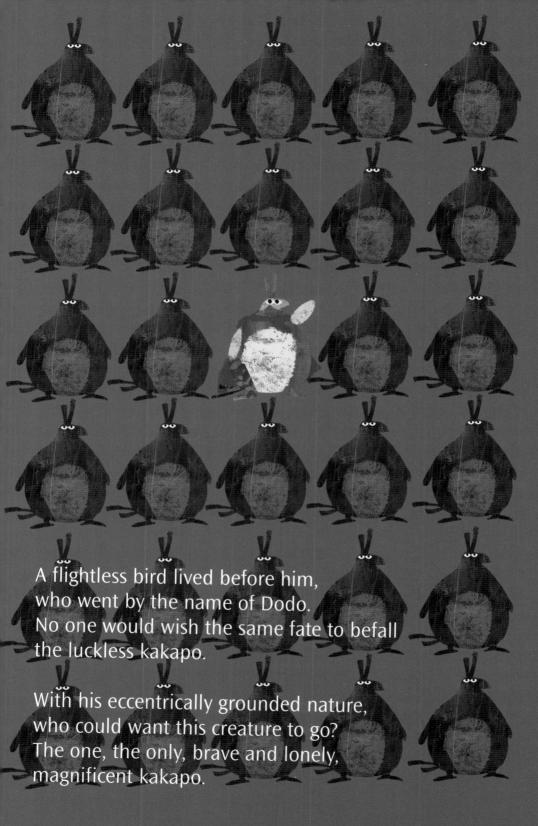

A flightless bird lived before him,
who went by the name of Dodo.
No one would wish the same fate to befall
the luckless kakapo.

With his eccentrically grounded nature,
who could want this creature to go?
The one, the only, brave and lonely,
magnificent kakapo.

Published in 2019 by Douglass Day
douglassday.com

First printed in 2019
Copyright ©
Dan Douglass has asserted his right under the copy, Designs and Patents Act 1988 to
be identified as the author of this work.

A catalogue record for this book is available from the British Library.

ISBN 978-0-9957588-9-6